Precious Gifts

Shakti Chionis

ISBN: 978-1-4834-1122-4 (sc)
ISBN: 978-1-4834-1123-1 (e)

Lulu Publishing Services rev. date: 7/28/2014

Dedication

My wish for the world. I wish that each human heart is seen for just how precious it is. We are all a collective spirit and if one person has it, we all have it. Claim it, own it, be inspired by it. Live authentically, live creatively, live joyfully with knowing the essence of preciousness is within all of us.

May all beings have happiness and the causes of happiness. May they be free from suffering and the root causes of suffering. May they never be separate from the great happiness devoid of suffering. May they live in the great equanimity free from passion, aggression and partiality.

Foreword

Every once in awhile, someone writes something that strikes a universal cord. A particular longing we have not had words for bears down upon our collective soul, until a writer finds the words, gifts them to us, and offers us a path back to ourselves. The book you are reading is such an example. Consider it a sacred document, a holy manuscript, a safe place for your tears to land, a sanctuary, a refuge. Allow the poetry to hydrate the arid places. Gaze upon the art and find its personal relevance to you. *Precious Gifts* calls on us, urges us, begs us, whispers to us to wake up to one simple truth - that of the *preciousness* of our own heart. Through poetry, prose, and art, Shakti Chionis guides us to this inner realm where all manner of possibility unfolds...when we simply choose to honor the preciousness of our own hearts.

We are at a tender place in the evolution of our species when awakening to the wisdom of the heart is crucial. As we wade through scores of information and data, emails and texts, we are hungry for the simple power of living from the intelligence of the heart. May it open you ever more fully to your own preciousness.

Angela Montano,
teacher, speaker, counselor
founder of ReThinkPrayer.com
and author of the forthcoming book
ReThink Prayer

Author's Note

"Love recognizes no barriers. It jumps hurdles, leaps fences, penetrates walls to arrive at its destination full of hope."

Maya Angelou

The Precious gift of life is contained inside each of our hearts. We all are precious, and we are all (as a collective) on the same journey. EVEN, if we don't believe it. We are all connected, and we are all human. Humanity must come to accept this as a whole.

The human heart is seeking this. Society is begging for this. It doesn't matter what language you speak, what color you are, what gender you are and even what religion you practice. Learning to show up in life, learning to be brave enough and step into your courage is growing throughout humanity. We are all being asked to be brave enough to become our authentic selves. The human spirit requires this for sustenance, and the human heart breathes this for existence.

So many of us are hearing our calling. Hearing that it's time to be seen for who we are and live authentically. Allow your precious gifts to enter the world and be seen. We all have room, and we all have something to share. It's time to make a difference in the world around you. It's time to grow and expand into your truth and open your hearts.

Table of Contents

Author's Note   5

Introduction   7

Acknowledgements   9

The Power of Failure- We Get to
Decide what it Means   10

10 Commandments of Self Love   16

I Radiate Self Love   17

Just one   18

I allow change   19

Pain   20

Letting Go   22

The Way of the Warrior   23

I am Unconditional Joy   24

The Mirror   25

The Remarkable Forces of Nature   27

Movement......Remembering Fearlessness   29

Wings on a Prayer   30

Breathing....Oxygen fuels the mind and spirit!   31

Sweetness of Life   34

Thank you Thank you   35

Listen to the Whispers   37

Promises   38

Blessings Everywhere   39

Believing in Myself...Nature's Gift   41

What does it take?   42

LOVE   43

Acceptance- Nature's Healing Remedy   44

No More Tears   45

It only takes a moment   45

Like a Kaleidoscope   46

I am a Magician   47

I am at peace   47

The Gift   48

Freedom   52

Introduction

I am ever changing in my personal growth. I have found that for as long as I can remember, I have been reaching....reaching for something that I believed was attainable and yet could not be seen. Reaching far out to the stars themselves, wishing I would catch one. Decades of wanting to become who I am meant to be. BELIEVING that I can attain it and make it part of my everyday life. Living authentically and finding joy in the moments of my day and embracing love. It has come with a lot of tears and lots of perseverance. It has brought me many questions, many fears and many a day that I lost sight of who I am.

Self-expression has always come through my hands as an extension of my heart. Even as early as 5 years old, painting was a peaceful time for me. In my 20's, I worked with my hands as a pastry chef and a floral designer. My desire to create beauty has always been a part of my soul's desire. The first passage, The Power of Failure, I believe to be the most powerful time in my life of both innocence and desire. Together, those combined created many life lessons which have followed me for decades. May my experience and wisdom bring insight and grace into your life.

I have always been clear about one thing. That my heart is precious. That my life is precious. That I have spent a life of vulnerability because I see beauty in the simplest things and am touched deeply by flowers, music, nature and humanity. Deep from within I have endured such obstacles knowing that I may overcome them in this lifetime. This book is a journey of self-love. It was born from a year of asking the question "What would someone who loves themselves do? And following through with whatever my intuition would say. Precious Gifts has been created from that place of inspired action. My hope is that it will inspire you. My gift to you is to nourish and bathe you in truth. Truth of the heart and truth of Consciousness. We are all walking in the same direction but sometimes we are following someone else's path. Allow these passages to shed light in areas of darkness and to bring life to you where you have been lost. You are beautiful, and I love you. May the "Essence of a Precious Heart" awaken within.

♥♥♥

Acknowledgements

Special thanks to my husband who has endured the emotional roller coaster that I ride on. Without him, I wouldn't be practicing my life's work. I want to thank all my friends that have supported me in my journey, both spiritual and physical. Thank you to my spiritual teacher, Thrangu Rinpoche, for giving me the perfect path to embrace and practice in my lifetime. Thank you to my dear friend and Tibetan Doctor, Nashalla Nyinda, for her healing work and helping me recover from traumas in my lifetime. Without her, the healing of my body wouldn't feel so complete. Thank you Kevin Lee, one of the most important angels in my life, for caring enough about me in my youth. Thank you to my editor, my copyeditor, my publisher, my children for letting me take time to write and create. I am very grateful for all the healers I have worked with and all the teachers that have guided me on my journey of walking into love, walking my path of surrendering and vulnerability and embracing my precious heart within. I am profoundly grateful to Divine Intelligence for the continued support of bringing exactly what I need when I need it. I feel so many blessings, thank you.

♥♥♥

The Power of Failure- We Get to Decide what it Means

Why does this affect me so? What am I feeling? Sheer Anger! Total disgust with myself. Hatred and disappointment in my life stain my thoughts. Why? Because in my ego's opinion, I should already be who I am meant to be, and I am *not* there! Not by a mile.

I feel so much disgust. My fears and resentment have grown into hatred and pain. I am at a loss for who I never became. Full of shame, I see that I have wasted my life—*or so I perceive it that way.*

It is hard to accept this. I am so sorry that I have failed so frequently at empowering myself. Seriously, what extremes must I take to wake up and say, "I am finally okay with myself; I am here, warts and all"?

Instead, life has molded me, shaped me, and created me where I am right now.

Tears of anger fill my eyes. Why pursue so many times my desire to make something of myself? What *am* I making?

What did I expect to have happened already? Who did I think I was supposed to be? Fear, disappointment, and sadness shadow me as I have moved on.

Now I am asking myself, "What would someone who loves themselves do?"

It struck me, what if I decided to define what I believe I failed at? As I looked at my life, what I perceived as success and failure started to unravel.

I was learning how I defined each of these two words. This was a monumental moment for me.

Because I experienced my power at a young age of believing I could do anything, believing that I could make anything happen, I concluded in my late twenties, as one dead end led to another, that I couldn't maintain, sustain, or become successful at what I really wanted.

Attempts to open a restaurant failed as investors backed out. My joy and passion as a pastry chef failed at so many corners, it drove me mad. As a successful pastry chef in Chicago, my experience in my move to Seattle changed my belief.

Several jobs within a year, eventually attempting to do something on my own, I faced many frustrations. With enthusiasm from being told I was one of the best vegan pastry chefs around, I thought I could make a success of myself—and yet, no one would hire me. *Why?*

Was it not clear just *how much* I was dedicated to making this happen? Was it not understood that I used my last cent to give it my best shot? Penniless, having moved five times in one year, dealing with a car accident and my dog running away brought me to one dead end after another. I finally surrendered, and gave up.

When I reflect back on my life, I can see that if I had succeeded in these endeavors, I never would have worked

on my own healing and opened up to my own gifts as a healer. Fate or destiny had another plan for me.

My definition of failure became clear to me. It didn't help that I believed I could not make much money. (Or was it that I believed I wasn't worth a lot?)

Because I lacked the skillful means to ask for help, needed to improve my coaching skills, and had minimal computer skills, I felt like I didn't have the strength to sustain anything on my own (especially as resources back then were considerably different than what they are today).

I felt it had all led me down a big black hole that I defined as failure.

Then one day I sat down and made a bullet list showing all the failures on one side and all the successes on the other side. All of a sudden I had a light bulb moment where it was clear that I had more successes than I ever thought.

I began seeing my strengths. Looking at my failures and successes this way has changed the charge I have on it. I'm not afraid of ideas, or starting something and making something out of nothing. This is *not* failure!

As I continued looking and decoding my thoughts, I could see that I connected my self-worth and self-esteem with money and earnings in my definition. That is *not* success. That is all about old beliefs and being stuck in them.

I have changed in twenty years. And now, I can see how different I am. My past is not my future. My worth is not based on money, talents, or what I have proven to myself or

the world. Success is not a destination; it is how we choose to live our life on a daily basis.

I can only now see this. At a young age, there was no way I could see it..

Life needs to create "failures" so we have two viewpoints to reference from.

I've recognized that I am quite successful at many things. As I looked at my successes on my bullet list, I realized that I need to market my strengths and hire someone for the things I'm not great at. Maybe even get a coach. As my excitement bubbled up, for the first time in my adult life, I felt I was becoming myself.

By redefining this word "failure," I learned that I am able to move forward and embrace who I am becoming. The guilt, the anger, the wishes and desires that shadow my past can fade away.

The illusions of who I was and who I am can fade as my authentic self emerges and rises above. I get to create success now through my choices. I can rejoice that I have made it thus far. For me, that is magical. I feel I am enough.

That is how someone who loves themselves gets to decide what failure means.

Dew drops of kindness,
heal the heart's broken pieces.

~

Open eyes see beyond,
Open hearts look within.

~

Aim high if you wish to plant seeds of
compassion.

~

I only make authentic choices in my life.
I free myself to be who I am.

Let it be said the wish fulfilling peace is inside.
Like the million stars glittering in the dark of the night.

Let the hope and prayers for all beings to be free from
suffering be wished upon as magic and miracles, as each
star shines for each sentient being, bringing peace to all.

Let there be a song sung in the spirit of all that is. A
song that ignites faith, passion and springs life into the
awakening heart.

Change your mind
Change your heart
Live your dreams.

---

10 Commandments of Self Love

1. *Be Brave and courageous*
2. *Be Honest*
3. *Be True to yourself*
4. *Be Proud*
5. *Be Happy*
6. *Be Joy*
7. *Be Kind*
8. *Be Loving*
9. *Be Forgiving*
10. *Have Faith and Believe*

Joyful expression
Brilliance expand.
Inside the heart
power thrives,
Fill up and reach out.
Give away,
There's nothing more to do.

I Radiate Self Love

The swirl of internal winds rush upward.
Warmth, heat, love ~ penetrate.
Inside I melt away the cold dark days.

High up above the birds soar.
I open my wings. I take flight.
I am finding my way home.

What a miracle.

♥♥♥

Just one

**All it takes is just one new thought.
Run with it.
It will change your world.**

Affirmations

*I give thanks for my immediate and complete emotional
healing under grace in perfect ways.*

I deserve success, and I accept it now.

I deserve love, and I accept it now.

I believe in myself, and I accept it now.

♥♥♥

<u>I allow change</u>

I open the window and climb through.
Leaving behind sorrow and fear.
I wipe my tears.

Pain

The lost soul of eternity will belong to the Heart of King.
I am your soul talking. I am your flame. I am your cousin
of truth.

Let me tell you.
Let me share a story.
You were born free.
Free to live a Heart filled life.
You were born to love, laugh, cry and let joy drink from
the fountain of youth.

The first time you cut me down, I cried.
Then it was not the same. You shunned me away.
Aching at your loss, you don't speak to me anymore.
Lost in a world of flames-

You ignite anger with your breath.

Words sting.
Words bite.
Words kill.

Be still and smolder out.
Be lifted from the blaze.
Anguished with heat, you must find the way to seek help.
Burnt to a crisp, it's time to transform.

Rise above and yield to me.
I hold the key for your sanity.
Rise above, float along, you need never to endure such
anguish again.

Rise to the joy.
Rise to the stars.
Be free at last.
Be free to be me.
Rejoice in your calling.
Be home at last.
Be honor.
Be love.

Be home at last.

♥♥♥

Would you rather be 'oh so smart' or 'oh so kind'? The world needs us to let go of our 'oh so right' and allow our compassionate hearts to heal the world.

Being brave is just another aspect of one's courage. Start small and grow into your courage and strength. No one said you had to start big. I give you permission to start where you are. One baby step at a time and before you know it, you will be running.

~

*As I am inspired, I inspire others.
As I am fed inspiration, I feed others inspiration.*

~

As I say Yes to the universe, the universe says Yes back to me.

~

Positive words and positive actions grow, everyday in every way.

Letting Go

*Only now I see the master plan.
It changes day by day.
Be present, and you will find~
You are the miracle* today.*

The Way of the Warrior

On you go, Relentless through the night.
A battle, a plague, a rich life of fear and pain.
Going to battle you say? The ego wants to win.
Wake up! Wake up! Don't be fooled. The trickster is
tricking you again!
Wake up! Master, Master, look around. Life is what you
make it.
Great beauty surrounds us. Great bliss imbues us. It's
all for the taking right now!
Become a warrior- Wake up! Wake up! Do not let ego
win. There is much to be done. The world welcomes you
on your journey. We are all walking home.
Namaste.

<u>I am Unconditional Joy</u>

To be present enough to allow the freedom of life to make magic. To give freely. To give love unconditionally. To be enthusiastic. To jump with pure joy at the moment I enter my own soul. I lift my head with power and speak my authentic truth. I have taken my joy and transformed it into pure awakening of spirit's essence. I get to be life incarnated as the essence of bliss.

Let my spirit Soar!

The Mirror

Outside the barrier of extremes,
live the light consciousness of Divine Love.
Drop into silence.
Thoughts arise, thoughts cease.

Coming and going.
Illusions are just mere appearances.
Now what?
No matter where you are, there you are.
Nothing to hide, no one hiding.
Where do I go? There is no where to go.
All is perfect~ and in emptiness I live.

The Remarkable Forces of Nature

In the beginning of time, nature was just a force of what is. It truly is energy, and it remains just that. But nature has evolved with evolution and man intertwining. The realms of what is and what was "appear" different. Ultimately the separation of the two remain the same.

What makes the forces of nature so profound? Is it that we can't see it? Or understand it? Or is it that we deeply know it internally and choose to not be part of it. Are we scared to be that powerful? Choosing to deny our own forces is choosing to avoid this universal truth of energy.

We are all made up of energy. We are all thought forms. We have made this agreement to dance with both and manifest as humans into what we perceive as relative truth. Our nature of minds live in both worlds - one eye seeing above and one eye seeing below. Each time we separate these two aspects, we observe separation.

If we choose to allow them to live comfortably together, we will enjoy moments where we can see the union of these two living and breathing together. Being able to experience a "Oneness", so to speak. The illusion of separation no longer exists, for we are in union with all that is.

We are in union with the universal truths of energy and thought forms. Decide which world you want to breathe in. Your life will reflect it.

Suffering is living an illusion of separation of all that is. Miracles are living a moment of oneness with all that is. They ARE the same coin. Flipping it will not matter. Allow your eyes to see that even the coin is an illusion and that ultimately we are all forces of nature. What choice did you make today? What would someone who loves themselves choose?

Movement......Remembering Fearlessness

I remember pedaling my bike down hill, going as fast as I could. The freedom in that speed, the wind in my face. The fearlessness of being free, with no worries at all.

I remember the feeling of ice skating across the ice with power in my legs, especially when I would skate backwards. The freedom I had to move quickly, gracefully and with great speed. The breeze once again washing over me. Fearlessness overcame me when I would jump and spin. One of my greatest joys in life.

I remember dancing with endless desire of moving my body to rhythm. Spinning, tapping, flying across the floor to the beat of sound. What amazing joy I felt. The freedom of movement, without a care in the world.

I remember skate boarding down the streets in my home town. Speed and power combine in the fearless act of being a kid. No worries at all. No one could stop me, for I was invincible. The joy of power, strength and speed combined. How amazing!

When we are young life is infinitely full of freedom and fearlessness. Joy just is a natural state.

Don't let life change us so much that we get trapped in fear. Trapped in an aged body that forgets all the joy we once breathed. Even though they are just memories now, I still believe that freedom is within my reach.

Let that be my my miracle now.

♥♥♥

Wings on a Prayer

Fly into the breeze.
Catch the sun ablaze.
Float onto a cloud and
jump into a realm of possibilities.

Climbing high up,
Find the opening,
to which we catch the heavens above
and seek guidance.

Love each other
Pray we find peace. Another peak is around the
bend.
The moment we let the heart
open, we win!

Breathing....Oxygen fuels the mind and spirit!

What is inspiration? It is being in spirit. What is bringing in the spirit? It is your breath. Breathing is taken for granted. It literally is something we can do without thinking. We can do it in our sleep, in a coma and even when we are in panic.

It won't be the first time you forget that this is one of the most important aspects of living. Without breath, we can not live. Without living, we are dead. *However, what level of living are you expecting in your life? Treading water? Suffocating? Thriving? Are you happy with the level of life support you sustain in right now?*

What forms the breath? It is a subtle kind of wind that moves through us. *Consciousness* is another form of wind that moves through us until we die, and then it passes out of our bodies. *Does that mean our breath is consciousness? Does that mean breathing literally is the aspect of who we are? Are they inseparable?*

Now, let's look at wind. What is wind? It is an element of

energy and force that come together to make movement. Wind is no different then our breath. What is moving the wind? It's another subtle form of energy that I suspect matches that of consciousness. *So does that mean, the winds around us are alive? Does it mean that all forms of consciousness are surrounding us?* We are therefore existing in a vortex (or a hologram) of subtle energies that move outside, inside, and literally in a secret form of all that is.

What does this have to do with life? Breath? Living? *It means that every level of being, exists in some kind of consciousness.* Therefore, every action you take is measured in some aspect of consequences. Karmic seeds are planted on every realm of existence. This literally creates your life.

You are born from consciousness. A seed grows through the energy, and forces of subtle winds create a human. That energy is connected to you at every level of your being. In that observation, allow yourself to live consciously. Allow yourself to become the winds of reality.

Let life move you in the direction you are meant to grow. There isn't any need to resist what is.

Just like in nature, life grows naturally. Resistance doesn't exist. Energy flows around and allows nature to just exist in a state of natural bliss. Haven't you noticed when you are in nature, you get fueled by "oxygen" and "inspired" by nature's presence? At the top of a mountain, you gain vast perspective and are fueled with greater awareness in spirit and in consciousness.

By a bubbling brook, or a water fall, you are filled with energy. You are filled with "life". You are filled with renewal (which oxygen brings us in great quantities).

Walking in a meadow of flowers, a garden, a rainbow of colors. All healing aspects filling your visual, your sense of smell, and allowing your body to align with the natural energies of life.

We find we relax more, we are at peace more, and we can allow ourselves to just rest in our natural state. *Oxygen is a powerful form of healing, because it is a form of consciousness.*

All these levels of consciousness help us to be alive. They help align us back to our natural state of bliss. When the stress of life is catching you in a mouse trap, look for the winds of all kinds.

Look to see where your consciousness can be fueled.

Your mind and your spirit are what sustain the body. Without these forms of winds, we would be dead. These are what keep us going. How do you want to sustain them? How do you want to move in life? Find ways to keep allowing yourself to open and remain balanced so spirit can continue to live inside in ways that bring expression, expansion, awareness, growth, bliss and inspiration. You never know what the subtle winds are calling you to do. As my friend, Jacob Lieberman, says, *"What if life is looking for you?".*

"If today was the first day of the rest of your life, what would you choose to be?" Make it the most important day of your life, because it is literally the only day of your life. *Today is now.* Tomorrow is not here, and yesterday is already gone and too late to be something else, since you have already planted those karmic seeds.

All these seeds lie dormant until they ripen. And you never know which life time they will sprout.

Feed your mind spirit. Drink it in like an elixir. Be inspired, as often as you can, and fuel your mind. It literally is what is keeping you alive right now.

Breath is your master. Breath is your life force. Make a difference in your life today.

Live magically, live consciously and allow yourself to live with love inside. Divine love surrounds you in the vast world of all that is. What more can we ask for? It seems like bliss is already here, just allow it.

♥♥♥

Sweetness of Life

Look for the sweetness in life.
Let it fill you up as you drink it in.
Let is satisfy every cell in your being,
as it nurtures you
and your deepest hearts desire.

Thank you Thank you

I am grateful for my eye sight, for It has given me the beauty to see the riches of life, color, and all the masterpieces life creates.
How lucky I am.

I am grateful for my ears, for they have gifted me the beauty of music and the joyful sounds of laughter to hear.
How lucky I am.

I am grateful for my nose, for it has gifted me the delightful smells of fragrant flowers and wonderful foods we eat.
How lucky I am.

I am grateful for my taste, as it has gifted me the delicious foods I eat. What simple joy to delight in our bounty of food.
How lucky I am.

I am grateful for my touch for it has gifted me a feeling of connection. It has gifted me the ability to express myself through my hands, where I can paint, write, heal, hug, hold, etc...what shear delight.
How lucky I am.
Yes, what a precious life I have. I am lucky.
Thank you. Thank you.

Listen to the Whispers

Hold me in your arms. Open the love in my heart.
Eager for more - Sink into the healing mantra
To the song of the heart.

Praise the Gods/Goddess's for freedom of hatred.

Live in the moment and walk into emptiness. Let the heart heal.
Let the mind find peace.

Listen to the whispers open to the melody of the unseen.
Embrace your song deep inside.

Listen to the whisper.

Eat, sleep, pray, listen to the joy filling our hearts.
Open to the magic. Believe in the miracle.
We pray, we sing, we eat, we sleep, we wake and hope we are
blessed with one more day.

Listen to the whispers.

Love yourself.
They sing the song of joy deep inside.
Let that be enough.

Written during a full moon
drum circle, summer 2013.

Promises

It never mattered how much a wish was, when promises were never kept.

To dream and believe in a wish come true, what matter that my wishes were dreams unfulfilled, stories untold?

What matters most are the dreams I live. The stories become the wishes filled and the memories of dreams once lived.

♥♥♥

Blessings Everywhere

I identify with success.

I identify with joy.

I identify with greatness.

To all my readers, I just wanted to shower you with lots and lots of blessings today.

You are blessed and blessed and blessed with the spirit shining in each and every one of you. May divine love flow through you today, overflowing your cup with greatness. Great joy and love fill you, your surroundings, your children, your work, your families, your whole life and spread throughout to your community and all interactions with those you know and those you may never even know. I praise you in all of your glory and spirit of who you are. Make magic and miracles today in your life as you engage. Be a loving presence. May you have peace of mind and peace in your heart all day long. You are all a blessing on this planet, and you each have a unique gift to offer the world. Believe in yourself, believe in humanity, believe in the greatness of all that is.

The heart knows perfect love. The heart lives authentically and opens when we surrender into this love.

Believing in Myself...Nature's Gift

Lift the head high.
Open your eyes and look inside.
Perhaps you do not see what I see.
Perhaps you are blinded by ignorance.

Lift the head high.
Open your eyes and look inside.

Breathe, Relax, Trust, Open

Instead of closing down, lift your head high
and believe you are safe. There is only
beauty, sunshine and greatness. Magic sits
inside and you are the creator of Glory, Joy and Great
LOVE.

Breathe, Relax, Trust, Open

Letting in great hopes and dreams becomes your new
reality.
In gratitude and faith your heart lives and breathes such
joy.

Let today be lived as if it were your best day ever.
Then do it again and again and again.

♥♥♥

What does it take?

To grow up.
To become the person you believe you can be.
To grow wings and take flight.
To open your heart and relax with what shows up.
To learn lessons the easy way instead of the opposite.

It takes forgiveness. It takes patience. It takes flexibility.
It takes faith.

But most importantly it takes showing up. There's magic
in just showing up.

Being yourself, being authentic, being humble and being
loving....
What would someone who loves themselves do?
Be present.

LOVE

I love the gentle breeze kissing my cheek.

I love the radiance of the majestic tree that stands tall beside me.

I love the sound of joy ringing in my ear.

I am joy. I am love. I am blessed.

Thank you kind world for teaching that I am more than enough.

♥♥♥

Acceptance- Nature's Healing Remedy

Listening to my story today. Wishing I could have done better. Small steps of successes with big regrets of anger. Wishing I could have done better. Feeling sorrow. Acceptance feels like a balm. Tomorrow I pick up my feet and look for more successes. They are always there. Washing my hands of the stains I made on my son today. Acceptance of what is. I will say prayers and wish more successes tomorrow. Breathe in and out, I accept my actions. I allow for new choices tomorrow.
I'm sorry.

~

You are cherished. You belong here.
And I love you. It's never too late to live.

♥♥♥

No More Tears

All my grief, All my tears,
All my suffering from beginningless time, I forbid you
to be my keeper, I forbid you to take me away.
No one will ever take my worth again. Nothing will ever
take my stand away. No one will ever claim me.
Nothing will hold me back ever again.
I am Love.

~

Drop by drop the flower sheds it's petals.
One by one....
Letting the ripening of fruit fill with sweetness.

~

It only takes a moment

A moment to say yes,
A moment to say I love you,
To embrace with a hug,
To be ok with who I am....right now.
Letting peace be.

Like a Kaleidoscope

A rainbow of 1,000,000 fractals is lighting my path.
A rainbow of patterns that reflect the basic nature of myself.
The magic sits in the hidden thoughts I once had into the becoming and dream like stage.
I am forever changed.
Magic, miracles and more bless me 1,000,000 times again and again.

♥♥♥

I am a Magician

It's not what you think.
It isn't the wonder of my mind.

It's the energy of the dakinis -
if what you want isn't there,
look elsewhere.

The mind alludes to what you see.
It's all there.
No one sees this level of magic unless you believe.

Look inside. It's all there!
Everything is there, if you just believe.

~

I am at peace

I am at peace with everyone I meet.
I am at peace with everything I do and say.
I am at peace with my self, my thoughts and my beliefs.
I am at peace and I accept it now.
And I prosper greatly,
because I believe I am worthy of it all.

The Gift

Music sings as the sound of the harp strikes my fingers.

They play on and on till the sun sets, and dips down into the earth.

Laughing echoes in the rooms as children play and play and play.

Water flows down the stream and tickles my toes as I stand inside it.

The melody of my soul bursts through my precious heart as I dance my song.

Spinning and spinning I dance my journey, on and on I go.

Laughing and playing as the music sings, striking my precious heart as I dance the song of my soul.

What is a gift? Are we giving or receiving? And if so, do we even truly know what that is?

Receiving....To accept and embrace whole heartedly is like drinking in the sweetness of life. Let it fill you up as you drink it in and let it satisfy every cell in your being as it nurtures the depths of your spirit. Then on it goes and fills your lungs. Next, spirit enters your in-breath, taking life force in and being inspired completely. Embracing the moment of gratitude.

Saying Thank you, Thank you, Thank you.

The gift of life. This precious human life we have. Do we take it for granted? If so, is it because we believe it is free? We watch humanity detach value to it and out of lack of appreciation, we abuse it, we neglect it, we devalue it, we numb it and we lose faith in spirit. Until something happens and we wake up and remember just how important we all are.

Giving.... Unconditional giving. To give without expectations. Who are we giving to and what motivates us? Oh the promises we once had, both secretly and spoken, to find that time just gets lost. We give to our children, do they realize the gift? We give to our friends and charities, but do we think it must cost something?

The best gifts of all are those that are often free. A smile from a stranger, a hug to a child, a precious moment, and of course love doesn't require any cost, but it doesn't mean anything if you hide it, shut it down, reject it and lose faith in it.

Giving unconditionally, having no expectations, that is a gift. Being present, honoring the person you are with,

listening without judgement, loving whole heartedly is a gift that is immeasurable.

Mother earth nurtures us all. Her spirit lives inside all of us giving and receiving daily. One of the most precious gifts of all. Life's essence of support, sustenance and our very existence of embodiment.

"Spinning and spinning I dance my journey on and on I go. Laughing and playing as the music sings, striking my precious heart as I dance the song of my soul."

I whisper Thank you, Thank you, Thank you....on and on I go.

"When you hold on to your history, you do so at the expense of your destiny."

Bishop T.D. Jakes

♥♥♥

Freedom

Master Master I am yours.
Let me abandon my ego.
It's time to let go of my old beliefs.

Listen and Honor the Great Mystery.

Listen to the subtle winds.
Calling me.
Begging me.
Entraining me.

Home Again.

Let my spirit soar!

♥♥♥

Freedom exists within. It is up to you.

~

Change your thoughts,
       Change your life,
              Be your dreams.

~

I believe anything is possible.

~

About the Author

Shakti Chionis is a mother, healer, medical intuitive, mystic, artist, writer, and wholefoods culinary artist. Self-expression has always come from deep within her heart. Her creativity, enthusiasm and passion for life always inspires others. She lives in Bellingham, Washington with her husband and 2 boys.

Visit her blog, 365 Days...Expect a Miracle*
www.365daymiracles.com
or visit her website at
www.miraclesandmore.com
www.shaktichionis.com

Made in the USA
Middletown, DE
31 October 2015